Mak
HAP

Wé McDonald

SINGER

BY RYAN HUME

Lightswitch
LEARNING

150 East 52nd Street, Suite 32002
New York, NY 10022
www.lightswitchlearning.com

Educators and Librarians, for a variety of teaching resources, visit www.lightswitchlearning.com

Library of Congress Cataloging-in-Publication Data is available upon request.
Library of Congress Catalog Card Number pending

ISBN: 978-1-68265-579-5
ISBN: 1-68265-579-2

Wé McDonald by Ryan Hume

Edited by Lauren Dupuis-Perez
Book design by Sara Radka
The text of this book is set in Minion Pro Regular.

Printed in China

Image Credits

Cover: Newscom, Jackie Brown
Page 1: See credits for cover
Page 4: Getty Images (all)
Page 5: (middle) Getty Images; (top and bottom) McDonald Family Archive
Page 6: Getty Images, iStockphoto
Page 7: McDonald Family Archive
Page 8: McDonald Family Archive
Page 9: Getty Images, Fotosearch RF
Page 10: Kimeth McClelland
Page 11: (top) Getty Images; (bottom) McDonald Family Archive
Page 12: McDonald Family Archive
Page 13: Getty Images (top and bottom)
Page 14: McDonald Family Archive
Page 15: Getty Images, Hero Images
Page 16: Getty Images
Page 17: Getty Images
Page 18: McDonald Family Archive

Page 19: Getty Images, iStockphoto (all)
Page 20: Getty Images
Page 21: Wikimedia, Maud Cuney-Hare
Page 22: Steve Schnur
Page 23: Getty Images, iStockphoto
Page 24: McDonald Family Archive
Page 25: Getty Images
Page 26: McDonald Family Archive
Page 27: Getty Images, iStockphoto
Page 28: Steve Schnur
Page 29: Getty Images
Page 30: McDonald Family Archive
Page 31: Getty Images, Blend Images
Page 32: McDonald Family Archive
Page 33: McDonald Family Archive
Page 34: McDonald Family Archive
Page 35: Getty Images, iStockphoto
Pages 36-37: Getty Images
Page 38: Getty Images

Page 39: Getty Images
Page 40: Getty Images
Page 41: McDonald Family Archive
Page 42: McDonald Family Archive
Page 43: Getty Images, iStockphoto
Page 44: McDonald Family Archive
Page 45: Wikimedia, Christopher Peterson
Page 46: Jase Michael
Page 47: Getty Images
Page 48: (bottom) Getty Images; (top) Steve Schnur
Page 49: (bottom) Getty Images, Cultura RF; (middle and top) McDonald Family Archive
Page 50: McDonald Family Archive
Page 51: (both) McDonald Family Archive

"Success is when you enter this world and make a beautifully large impact, and leave a legacy behind."

Wé McDonald

. . .

Make It! HAPPEN!

Skills for Success

This recurring feature at the end of each chapter will help readers develop skills to enable them to achieve their goals. The "Make it Happen" content will tie relevant information from every chapter into ideas about career readiness. It will ask readers to make useful lists, blog posts, and charts that can help them in the future.

Contents

Introduction

Standing on a stage facing a crowd can be difficult. It can be stressful. Singing in front of judges who are going to decide if you are in or out is a challenge most people do not face. For Wé (pronounced "way") McDonald, it's just another step in her journey. A large part of her life is about music, but she is also so much more. Wé McDonald overcame bullying and harassment to become a finalist on NBC TV's *The Voice*. She is now an innovative jazz vocalist and pop singer. Wé has entertained millions with her extraordinary talent. Her story will help students discover the many career opportunities available in the music industry. Whether you perform onstage, work backstage, or run a recording studio, you take the **initiative** to succeed, and you do it as part of a team. It takes a lot of **collaboration** between people to put on a great show. Students will discover that success in the music industry is not easy. It means being disciplined, working hard, having a plan, and getting support from others.

Wé knew from the time she was very little that she wanted to be a performer.

In 2015, Wé performed at Lincoln Center in New York City.

1 Early Life

Even at six years old, Wé was showing interest in music and the arts.

Who is Wé?

There are more than 146,000 people living in Paterson, New Jersey.

Wé McDonald was born at Roosevelt Hospital in New York City on January 23, 1999. She lived with her family in a neighborhood called Harlem. It was a fitting place for the future singer to be born. It has been a center for African American art and music since the 1920s. At that time, Harlem was known for its **jazz** music. Jazz is an important part of music history. In the '20s, jazz musicians used pianos, guitars, bass guitars, trumpets, saxophones, and many other instruments to create a brand new sound. Jazz has also influenced Wé McDonald, and the unique music she has created as a new voice in pop music. At just 18 years old, Wé McDonald is aiming to take over the world of popular music through her innovations and unique style.

Wé first lived in Harlem, but she later grew up in Paterson, New Jersey, just across the Hudson River from New York City. Childhood had its ups and downs for Wé. But she had the loving support of her close-knit family to help her through. "My family has been really tight around me all the time," she said.

DID YOU KNOW?

In 1999, the same year that Wé was born, Beyoncé released her breakout album, *The Writing is on the Wall*, with Destiny's Child. Beyoncé had formed the group in 1990, when she was nine years old.

Wé's Family

Her family also helped inspire her to be a musician. Her mom and grandparents are singers. Her sisters also sing. There was always music playing in the McDonald household. This impacted Wé. Her dad liked to play jazz records at home. Some of his favorite jazz musicians were Dizzy Gillespie and Louis Armstrong. The first jazz singer that Wé remembers hearing was Sarah Vaughan, who also grew up in New Jersey. Sarah Vaughan was one of the greatest jazz singers of all time. Her voice was complex and could hit both high and low notes. People now say the same thing about Wé's voice.

Wé's father, Varleton "Mac" McDonald, is a public school educator. He is one of Wé's biggest influences, and they share a very tight bond. Her mom, Jackie, sells real estate. Wé has five older sisters. She also has a younger brother named Noah. He was five years old when Wé was on season 11 of NBC TV's *The Voice*, a popular reality-TV singing competition.

Wé's sisters and her brother all love music. They are her biggest supporters.

ALL ABOUT SINGING

jazz: a type of American music with lively rhythms and melodies that are often made up by musicians as they play

soul: music that combines R&B (rhythm and blues) and gospel music

funk: a type of popular music that has a strong beat and combines traditional forms of African American music (such as blues, gospel, or soul)

musical theater: a type of play in which singing and dancing play an important part

production: a show (such as a play or movie) that is presented to the public

amateur: a person who does something for pleasure and not as a job

syncopated: of, relating to, or having a rhythm that stresses the weak beats instead of the strong beats

vocalist: a singer

Wé's mom was also a huge influence on her musical tastes. "My mom, she definitely got me into **soul** [music]," Wé told FRP TV in a YouTube video. Just like jazz, soul is also an important form of music in African American culture. Soul music was often played by large bands with many different horns, guitars, and keyboards. Many classic soul songs have been "sampled" by hip-hop artists to form new background music to rap over. Sampling is when an artist uses a part of one song to make a completely new song.

Wé and her mom on a family vacation in the Dominican Republic.

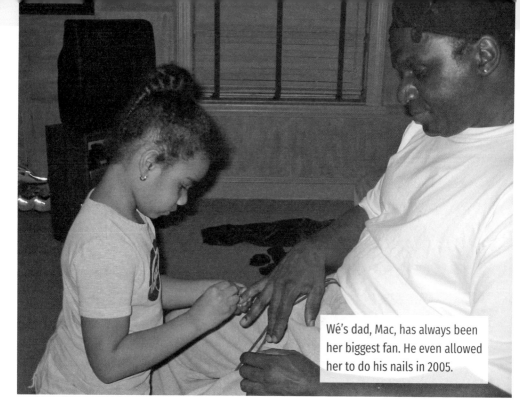

Wé's dad, Mac, has always been her biggest fan. He even allowed her to do his nails in 2005.

Music Diversity

Wé credits her parents for exposing her to so many different kinds of music from so many different musical eras. This influence is why Wé wants to be able to sing in a variety of different musical "genres." A genre is a type of music or art that can be classified by sharing similar elements or styles, like rock and roll.

"I don't want just to be able to do soul," she told FRP TV. "I do listen to a lot of hip-hop [and] pop, actually. I listen to a lot of country [and] a lot of alternative stuff. I feel like it gives me a new perspective on stuff." In that same interview, she went further, saying, "I sing wherever the soul is." Listening to a lot of different kinds of music can help singers find their own sound.

Superstar singer Michael Jackson also became one of Wé's major influences. His blend of soul, **funk**, and pop guided her musical tastes. Eventually, his success would heighten her career goals too. "And Michael Jackson [. . .]. If I'm a quarter of what Michael Jackson was, I've succeeded so much," she told the magazine *Teen Vogue*. "I'm always going to fight to be able to be one hundred percent of what he represented. Of course, I won't necessarily get to that point, but I will get as close as I can. I can only be myself. I can't be Michael."

Michael Jackson is famous for his unique sound and for his iconic dance moves.

DID YOU KNOW?

Michael Jackson had 13 number one hits as a solo artist. He also won 13 Grammy Awards in his lifetime.

New Jersey

New Jersey is the birthplace of many famous singers. Frank Sinatra, famous for singing "New York, New York," grew up in Hoboken, New Jersey, just across the river from Manhattan. Both jazz singer Sarah Vaughan and pop superstar Whitney Houston grew up singing in Newark, New Jersey.

Bruce Springsteen, who is called "the Boss," comes from Long Branch, New Jersey. Queen Latifah, actress and queen of old-school rap, is from Newark. The Fugees, a hip-hop group including singer Lauryn Hill, met each other in South Orange, New Jersey. Like Wé, rapper Fetty Wap lives in Paterson, New Jersey.

Diligence

Wé's name means "diligence" in Swahili. This language is native to Kenya and other African countries. The word diligence means hard work, effort, or determination. From a very early age, Wé was willing to show the world how diligent she could be as she set out to follow her dreams. She told *Essence* magazine, "When people ask me 'What do you wanna do?' I always say 'I wanna be one of the world's greatest entertainers and [never] stop.' I have to make sure I keep going."

At four, Wé's love of dress-up and performance was focused in acting classes.

Wé started school early, at the age of four, around the same time she started acting classes. "My parents saw that I was pretty active and really animated, and they were like, 'You need to use this beautiful energy and get into it. Do something productive.' It was either going to be acting or sports, and my mom wanted me to do acting so we did acting."

Wé's family has always been a driving force behind her ability to achieve her dreams. Their guidance has shaped who Wé is. Even when she was a little girl, they gave her the tools to succeed.

❝I wanna be one of the world's greatest entertainers and [never] stop. I have to make sure I keep going.❞

WÉ MCDONALD

DID YOU KNOW?

Wé's family gave her two nicknames: "WéWé" and "Wézer."

Make It! HAPPEN!

Research Your Interests

Turning something you love to do into a job can be a great idea. Whether you love to sing like Wé, write stories, or play video games, there are jobs that go with those interests. Share some of your favorite interests with a friend. Discuss your favorite parts of those interests. Now do some research.

- Search for a career with one of your interests in mind. Try typing into a search engine "Jobs for _____". Type your interest in the blank space.

- What type of jobs come up? Make a list.

- Search for jobs related to another interest. Are they similar? You may have interests that are very different, or ones that follow a similar path.

Share your potential job list with a parent or teacher. Together, you can brainstorm how to turn what you love into a possible future career.

2

First Steps of the Journey

The Apollo Theater opened in 1913. The theater can seat more than 1,500 people.

Exposure to the Arts

From a very young age, Wé has always loved to visit New York City, across the river from Paterson. Many new musical styles, like hip-hop and punk rock, began in New York City. From **musical theater** both on and off Broadway, to the New York Philharmonic, and the many street performers trying to make it big, music is alive in the city. "[New York City] was always my favorite place to go because if I knew I was going to New York, it was going to be something involving acting, dancing, and music," she says. "So I like to say that I grew up in New Jersey and New York." New York is also home to many historic live-music halls like Radio City Music Hall, Carnegie Hall, and the Apollo Theater.

Although she has spent her whole life in and around New York, Wé has never been to the Statue of Liberty, Ellis Island, or to the top of the Empire State Building. "I always think, 'I'm such a horrible New Yorker!'" she joked. But she has seen many of New York's classic music venues. Wé was 15 the first time she saw the inside of the Apollo Theater, and it surprised her. "Wow," she thought. "It looked so much smaller than I thought it would!" It had taken her many years of practice to see the inside of that legendary place.

There are more than 40 theaters located on Broadway.

Talent Show

Wé says she can't remember a time when she didn't love the arts. She says, "That was always something that I loved to do. When I was six I started playing piano. I started dancing at eleven. And I was twelve when I realized that I could sing and that I could actually make a career out of that. I told my dad, 'I want to sing.'"

Wé liked to sing along with her older sister Jasmine. They often sang karaoke at family barbeques. Wé would watch her sister perform at school talent shows and knew she wanted to sing too. She told *Teen Vogue* magazine in December 2016, "I would be like, 'I want to be up there with her and I want to sing with her and I want to be talented just like my big sister. I want to do that.'" She continued, "We actually sang an Alicia Keys song when I was in the third grade, maybe a little younger." Wé sang the song, "No One." Collaborating with her sister in front of the school was different for Wé than singing in front of the family. It was her first experience singing in front of a real audience.

In 2010, Wé practiced for a recital where she played a piece by Johann Sebastian Bach.

Find Your Voice Type

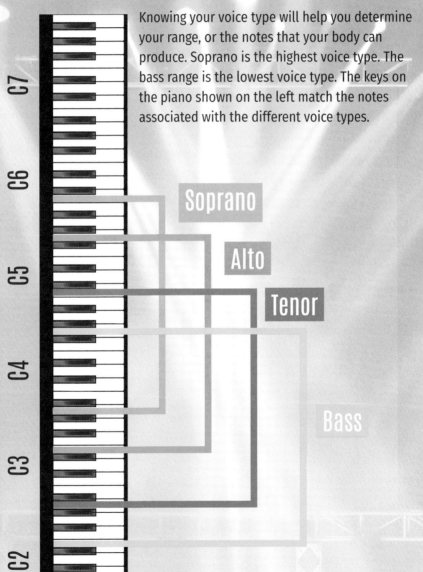

Knowing your voice type will help you determine your range, or the notes that your body can produce. Soprano is the highest voice type. The bass range is the lowest voice type. The keys on the piano shown on the left match the notes associated with the different voice types.

Soprano

Alto

Tenor

Bass

C7
C6
C5
C4
C3
C2

Becoming a Performer

Wé had her first experience performing in a musical when she was in the third grade. She was in a school **production** of *Annie*, a popular musical about an **orphaned** girl from New York who is adopted by a very wealthy man. Wé played Kate, one of Annie's orphaned friends. Along with the other orphaned girls, Kate sings in "It's a Hard-Knock Life." The girls dance through their terrible chores and sing about how hard it is to be an orphan.

The show *Annie* first appeared on Broadway in 1976.

Wé first began taking vocal lessons when she was 11 years old. Before that, she had been studying theater. But if Wé was serious about becoming a singer, her father thought she should enroll in an after-school program. So, she enrolled at Harlem School of the Arts in New York City. This gave her the opportunity to perform at places like Carnegie Hall and the Apollo Theater.

All of this diligence and practice landed Wé in front of one of the toughest audiences in the world at just age 16. **Amateur** Night at the Apollo Theater is famous for its crowd. The audience is encouraged to boo the performers off the stage. It's a **tradition**. Performers come from all over the world to try their luck. If the crowd doesn't like them, the booing will begin. If the boos get too loud, a siren will ring, and a stagehand, called "The Executioner," will appear. He dances the shamed performer off the stage. It's a wild scene, and performers need **self-confidence** just to try out.

"These are people from New York," Wé said. "They are going to boo if they want to boo! Before you even come on, people are thinking, 'I want to boo!' 'I want to boo!' … At other types of performances, people are going to have respect," Wé remembered. "It's not like they are going to boo you."

Backstage, the walls are painted black and covered with the signatures of past performers and guests. Everyone from Michael Jackson to Lauryn Hill to Barack and Michelle Obama have signed those walls.

Wé was horrified as she heard other performers get booed off the stage. "I was sixteen," she said, "but no one else knew that in the audience. So I was freaking out, like, I look like an adult! They're going to think I'm an adult! So they are going to judge me like an adult!"

Harlem School of the Arts

The Harlem School of the Arts was opened in 1964 by opera singer Dorothy Maynor. At the time she opened the school, Maynor noticed there were no opportunities for the children of Harlem in music and the arts. "What I dream of is changing the image held by the children," she once said. "We've made them believe everything beautiful is outside the community. We would like them to make beauty in our community." In 2017, Harlem School of the Arts celebrated its 50th Anniversary.

Amateur Night

Just offstage at the Apollo, there is a tree stump called "the tree of hope" that performers have been rubbing for luck since the 1930s. Wé gave it a rub and went out onto the stage.

This was her first time seeing the audience. "When you are on the stage, the audience looks larger than life." she said. "You look out into the audience and it's ridiculously gorgeous."

"The first thing I thought going out onstage was, 'I hope that I kill this,' and then I blanked out," she recalls. "I barely remember what the performance was like. All I remember was my family screaming and me crying at the end. And then I saw the audience meter and I got like a ninety-five."

For one of Wé's first place finishes, she sang "Listen" from Dreamgirls.

Wé took home first place that night. She went on to perform through all four rounds of the Amateur Night competition that year. She came in first place twice and second place twice. By facing her fears and singing her heart out, she made it all the way through one of the toughest talent competitions on the planet. Of course, it was just the beginning.

Make It! HAPPEN!

Write a Personal Essay

Stage fright is one of the most common fears that people have. However, having to speak and communicate to a group of people is very common in school and in many careers. Though you may not have sung in front of a large audience like Wé, you may have given a presentation in class, raised your hand to give an answer and had to speak in front of an audience, or been onstage during an assembly or school play.

- Write an essay about a moment when you were speaking or performing in front of a group of people.
- How did you prepare? Were you nervous? Did your hands sweat? Did your voice shake?
- If you love performing and speaking in front of an audience, explore why that may be.
- How did you feel afterwards? Did you communicate effectively? Relieved? Confident?

Think about the benefit of doing things that scare you. How have these experiences changed you?

3

Overcoming Obstacles

In middle school, Wé worked hard to make friends. This included joining sports teams.

Bullying is hurtful and unacceptable behavior.

Switching Schools

In the sixth grade, Wé moved to a small junior high school, far away from the school friends she had made growing up. From the first week at her new school, Wé was tormented and pushed around. Wé was getting bullied. "Everybody kind of knew each other already," she remembered. "There were kids that had grown up together since kindergarten, so they were already kind of cliquey. I was one of the few new people and I was already being ostracized." Bullying isn't always physical, but it does hurt people, whether it is done in person or online. A lot of bullying involves name-calling, making up rumors, or "ostracizing" people. To ostracize someone means to purposefully **exclude** and reject them in order to hurt them.

DID YOU KNOW?

About 28 percent of students in U.S. schools report being bullied at some point during their education. Most bullying happens in middle school.

Tough Beginnings

Within the first three days at her new school, Wé remembers being pushed, shoved, and called mean names by her classmates. Her parents went to her teachers and the principal, but nothing happened. The bullying continued.

Wé was lonely. She was bullied by her classmates for three years during junior high. She was even bullied about her high speaking voice. If you have ever heard her sing, you might be surprised to learn that Wé's natural speaking voice is very high. "There must be something wrong with me," she thought.

Wé's family tried to help her while she was being bullied. She felt stronger with their support.

Her father told *Essence* magazine, "Even when she was going through the tough times—she would come home

DID YOU KNOW?

Stars such as Zac Efron, Kate Winslet, Sandra Bullock, and Rihanna have all reported being bullied while growing up.

and tell us but one thing she didn't want to do, she didn't want me to pull her out of the situation," her father said. "She wanted to hold on and fight and challenge all of her obstacles." By doing this, Wé developed a level of strength and drive that toughened her up. This initiative prepared her to sing in front of large crowds.

Best-Selling Albums of All Time

The top 10 albums with the highest sales are all by artists who continue to sell records even decades after the album's release.

RANK	ARTIST	ALBUM	UNITS SOLD
1	Michael Jackson	*Thriller*	32 million
2	The Eagles	*Their Greatest Hits*	29 million
3	Billy Joel	*Greatest Hits Vol. 1 and 2*	23 million
4	Led Zeppelin	*Led Zeppelin IV*	23 million
5	Pink Floyd	*The Wall*	23 million
6	AC/DC	*Back in Black*	22 million
7	Garth Brooks	*Double Live*	21 million
8	Fleetwood Mac	*Rumours*	20 million
9	Shania Twain	*Come On Over*	20 million
10	The Beatles	*The White Album*	19 million

Finding Her Voice

When her father told her that he wanted her to go to an after-school program at Harlem School of the Arts, Wé had started crying. Explaining how she had felt, she said, "I didn't want to go into any more new places because I was horrified that the same thing was going to happen to me." Eventually she agreed to go, showing **flexibility**. "I ended up going and it was the best choice I ever made. That's when I started my vocal lessons and dancing."

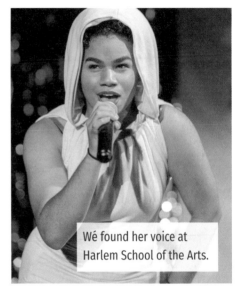

Wé found her voice at Harlem School of the Arts.

Not only was Harlem School of the Arts a great launch pad for Wé's growth as a vocalist and actress, but she also made lots of friends. She continues to stay in touch with the friends she made there. By the time she entered high school, Wé had put the bullying behind her, and instead focused on her acting, singing, and dancing. When asked what she would tell other kids who are being bullied, she said, "Be strong. These people aren't going to mean anything to you in the next four years. I promise."

Bullying does not just happen in high school. For Wé, one of the hardest things about working in the music industry is how much people focus on appearances. Industry people can be very critical. "As a singer in the music industry, people already look at you twisted, like you don't know what you are doing," Wé said. "People underestimate me because I'm a girl and the music industry is male run."

Wé has faced a number of personal criticisms as she follows her dream. "Someone has told me that I need to lessen the thickness of my vocals. I got told that by a vocal coach, and I was immediately disgusted. And I was like, 'What does that mean?'" She went on to mention, "I've been told that my hair is too big. I've been told that I need to straighten my hair if I'm going to make it."

The Fight Against Bullying

In 2017, students at Boca Raton Community High School in Boca Raton, Florida, started a club to combat bullying. The club is called We Dine Together. Bullying can often happen when students are alone outside of the classroom. The members of We Dine Together walk through the campus at lunchtime and ask to join other students who are sitting alone. Bullying happens less often when students are in a group. Not only are the members of We Dine Together making a difference, they are making new friends.

In Sherman Oaks, California, another student designed an app to prevent bullying. The app is called Sit With Us. The app allows student "ambassadors" to invite other students to come and sit at their table during lunch.

Music Industry Madness

Wé has grown confident in her style and sense of self. "When they look at me, they think that I have to be a Rihanna or a Beyoncé," she said. "And I'm like, I do dance. I will sing and I will say what I want to say."

One day when practicing in a studio, Wé was explaining some issues with a song to a band director. "I said, 'This song is so hard because it is **syncopated** and in sixth-eighths and I know that it's going to be difficult.'" As the band director listened to Wé's explanation, one of the male musicians turned around and said, "How do you know what that means? You're a singer." He was **implying** that he didn't expect a singer to know much about how music works.

Wé has developed a strong inner confidence, and she knows who she is. She often shows initiative in the face of different obstacles. She trusts herself to be herself. "When I meet somebody, I just lay it all out on the table," she said. "So if they want to run away, they can run away now. I figure I am meant to do this. And if it's meant to happen, the right person is going to understand where I am coming from. I just try to stay true to myself all the time whenever I speak, whenever I write [a song], because if you are writing, and you are not true to yourself, the song will not match up to how you feel and then it will never go anywhere."

Though Wé can transform herself with different hair or clothes, she knows who she is on the inside.

Make It Happen!

Make It HAPPEN!

Discover the Music Industry

There are plenty of jobs available in the music industry, both on the stage and off. Even if singing or playing an instrument is not your strongest skill, you can turn your love of music into an exciting career. Take some time and research each of the jobs listed below.

What do you need to start off in that position? What are the skills needed? How much is the starting salary? These are all important questions to ask.

- Record producer
- Recording engineer
- DJ
- Artist representative

Now that you know where your interests are, how can you prepare for a career in the music industry?

Wé's vocal coach, Ms. Yolanda Wyns, helps train Wé's voice for big events, like singing the national anthem.

Wé's Community

Even with all of her talent, Wé knows that she could not have made it this far all by herself. Many people have helped along the way. Wé's tight-knit family has always been supportive of her career. They have been there for Wé at every step along her journey. They were backstage at every performance she gave while on *The Voice*. Alicia Keys even invited Wé's family onstage following Wé's knockout blind **audition**. The whole family helped choose what songs Wé would sing for each of her performances on *The Voice*.

Alicia Keys helped prepare Wé for every new challenge *The Voice* presented to her.

Her time on *The Voice* showcased her great talent. *The Voice* brings together the strongest amateur **vocalists** from across the country. It has been broadcast on television since 2011. Through the process of

DID YOU KNOW?

The song "Feeling Good" was first popularized by jazz singer Nina Simone in her 1965 album *I Put a Spell on You.*

blind auditions, some of the most popular artists in music choose to coach amateur musicians based only on the sound of their voices. The show sent Wé's voice into more than 8 million living rooms. Her blind audition alone has also gathered more than 8 million views on YouTube. She is now well on her way to becoming a household name.

We's family rallies around her before every audition to help keep the jitters away.

Team Effort

We's father, Mac, has not only been a pillar of support, he is also her manager. A talent manager collaborates with an artist in every aspect of their career, including securing gigs, negotiating contracts, and choosing outfits to perform in. We has described her dad as very strict and serious. "He kind of trains me like how you would train an athlete," she said. As Mac told NorthJersey.com, his whole family learned that "if you want to be good at this, it's not about glamour and glitz, though that's a part of it, there's real work involved." You have to be responsible and be "committed to getting better, to understanding the business and staying focused."

In fact, her dad's help made all the difference in getting We her big break. At the time, We had been doing college auditions and had just gotten turned down by New York University. "I was freaking out," she said. However, her dad had a surprise. He had signed We up for *The Voice* auditions in Philadelphia.

We was already a big fan of the show. "Coming from my past, I thought, 'They don't know what you look like, they just go off what they're hearing.' And I think that's the most fair thing."

On the day of Wé's blind audition for *The Voice*, her parents, sisters, and brother tried to keep her in a positive mindset. Wé remembers her dad saying, "Stay focused. Make sure your voice stays warm. Don't pay attention to any of these people." Her mother, on the other hand, was very emotional. Wé remembers her saying, "Baby, you got this. You got this. You're so great, and I love you." Wé's sister took a different approach. "She was like, 'Don't mess up,'" Wé recalls. "And my little brother was in his own world, dancing around hoping he got filmed."

Throughout Wé's musical journey, another friend and **mentor** has also always been there. "My vocal coach, Ms. Yolanda, taught me how to sing with strength and not volume," Wé said. "She told me that insecurities shouldn't be holding me back, [they should be] building on the emotion of how I sing, and [I should be] defeating them with my success."

HISTORY OF SOUND

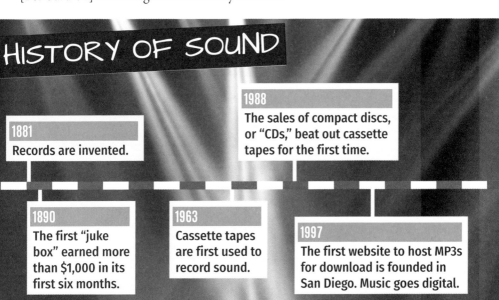

1881
Records are invented.

1890
The first "juke box" earned more than $1,000 in its first six months.

1963
Cassette tapes are first used to record sound.

1988
The sales of compact discs, or "CDs," beat out cassette tapes for the first time.

1997
The first website to host MP3s for download is founded in San Diego. Music goes digital.

Climbing the Charts

Understanding musical trends and cheering on fellow vocalists is an important part of starting a career in music. For a rising star, it's important to understand who you are competing with for the top spot on the music charts. Below are up-and-coming artists you can find on the radio and online.

TESSANNE CHIN

KINGSTON, JAMAICA · BORN 1985

Winner of *The Voice*'s fifth season, Chin performed a cover of Simon & Garfunkel's "Bridge Over Troubled Water." It was the first performance on *The Voice* to make it to number one on iTunes.

KEHLANI

OAKLAND, CALIFORNIA · BORN 1995

This R&B singer scored a Grammy nomination for her 2015 mixtape *You Should Be Here*. She followed her popular single "Gangsta" with the release of her first album in 2017.

H.E.R.

UNKNOWN

This mysterious R&B singer has released her debut music anonymously, without her name or image attached. H.E.R. stands for "Having Everything Revealed." There is a lot of buzz about this artist on social media, and many superstars, including Alicia Keys, love her music.

COBI

GRAND MARAIS, MINNESOTA · BORN 1986

This singer-songwriter found success with his single "Don't Cry For Me." He even landed an appearance on *The Tonight Show* with Jimmy Fallon, and performed at the Lollapalooza music festival in Chicago.

SUNDANCE HEAD

HOUSTON, TEXAS · BORN 1979

Head won season 11 on *The Voice*, beating out Wé and ten other contestants. In 2017, the country singer went on tour with Blake Shelton, his coach from *The Voice*.

Mentor and Friend

No artist has been as supportive of Wé's breakthrough as Alicia Keys, her coach on *The Voice*. During her blind audition, Wé's soulful rendition of Nina Simone's "Feeling Good" got the attention of all four judges, and she received a standing ovation. Since all four judges wanted to coach her, Wé had to pick one. Keys told her, "You came to this show to meet me." Keys continued, "I don't want to be like anybody else, and I don't want you to be like anybody else. You were born to show people what love sounds like." Hearing those words convinced Wé to pick Keys to be her coach.

DID YOU KNOW?

Alicia Keys's 2001 debut album, *Songs in A Minor*, went platinum five times over. For a record to go platinum it needs to sell one million copies.

Alicia Keys

Keys graduated high school at 16 and enrolled at Columbia University. She eventually left college to work on her music full time. She wrote all of the songs and most of the lyrics on her debut album, *Songs in A Minor*, and played all of the instruments. She eventually won five Grammys, including the award for Best New Artist. She was only 20 years old.

Her second album, *The Diary of Alicia Keys*, won six Grammy awards, proving that Keys was one of the most important artists of her generation. She has won twenty-two Grammy awards, sold over tens of millions of records, and started a film career. She has been a judge on *The Voice* since 2016.

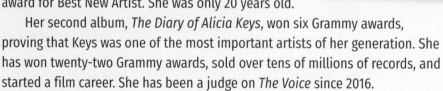

Make It! HAPPEN!

Audition for *The Voice*

It is important to prepare and practice for important auditions and other meetings with people, especially if you want to show your talents and skills. *The Voice* holds Open Call auditions in four cities across the country every year. But how do you get started?

- To audition you must create an Artist Account on their website (https://www.nbcthevoice.com/artistaccount/register)

- You can upload a clip of your singing for a chance to win a Beat the Crowd pass and avoid long lines (https://www.nbcthevoice.com/beatthecrowd)

- If you are under 18, you must have a parent or guardian present with you during the audition

- You must be 13 years or older to audition

If you can't audition for *The Voice*, can you audition or prepare for something else where you want to show people your talent and skills? Is there a school musical? Or a community theater that holds auditions? Ask a parent or teacher for advice.

5 Current Career

Since being on *The Voice*, Wé has gained a lot of recognition. In 2017, she was asked to perform at the G'Day Black Tie Gala in Los Angeles.

A Shining Star

Even before she appeared on *The Voice*, Wé was planning to take the music world by storm. She received the 2015 Clive Davis Future Music Moguls Merit **Scholarship**. Clive Davis is a famous record producer. He has worked with some of Wé's biggest influences,

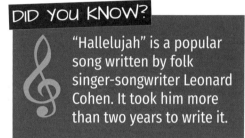

including Whitney Houston, Kelly Clarkson, Janis Joplin, and Alicia Keys. The Future Music Moguls Merit Scholarship gives high school students a behind-the-scenes look at making hit records today. It also shows them the financial aspects of the music business. It takes a lot of money to produce a hit record. You need to book studio time, hire musicians, and pay to create a final mix of the completed audio. This takes collaboration, **problem-solving**, and **communication** between the artist and the producer. Artists need to learn to work within their budget. Wé beat out around 700 other high school students from New York to get this great scholarship.

At Wé's first college audition, she sang Nina Simone's "Feeling Good."

New Opportunities

On *The Voice*, Wé eventually made it through the Battle Rounds and the Knockout Rounds to become a finalist. Unfortunately, Wé did not win the grand prize. She ended up placing third in season 11. However, the exposure has changed her life and has given her many new opportunities.

Speaking of her time on *The Voice*, Wé told NorthJersey.com that it was "a how-to-be-famous boot camp," where she learned how to extend herself as a performer. She also learned other valuable information about the television and recording industries. "I was actually relieved," Wé said of her third-place finish. "After a certain point, you don't really care what happens to you after that because I knew I was in the Top Four. I was going to be fine. I couldn't have been happier just to be there at that point."

For Wé, *The Voice* was a stepping stone to bigger things. She is grateful for her time there, but wants to make sure to keep moving forward.

"There were a lot of fans that had contacted me or commented and said that they were upset," Wé admitted about her third-place finish. "And a lot of family members that said that they were upset that I didn't win, but my really close circle, they were all really proud of me and they were supremely supportive."

By the age of 17, Wé became the only student at William Paterson University majoring in Jazz Vocals. This has given her the opportunity to continue improving her singing skills while getting her education.

Highest-Paid Female Solo Artists in 2016

Only a small group of superstar singers make it to the top of the charts. And even fewer make it to the top five highest-paid female vocalist list. All of these artists started out with big talent and the drive to succeed, just like Wé.

ARTIST	EARNINGS
Taylor Swift	$170 million
Adele	$80.5 million
Madonna	$76.5 million
Rihanna	$75 million
Beyoncé	$54 million

Wé was honored by the mayor of Paterson (in glasses) for representing her community so well.

What Next?

Just one month after she finished *The Voice*, Wé was given the key to the city of Paterson, New Jersey. This is a symbol of great honor given to someone who is important to the area. She sang "Hallelujah" in the city council chamber to celebrate the event. The mayor of Paterson, Jose Torres, named December 20, 2016, "Wé's Day" and said that Wé was "the voice of Paterson." His daughter, Joely Torres, a good friend of Wé's from high school, read off a list of her many accomplishments. "I think I am the youngest person to ever get the key to Paterson!" Wé said. That same month, all of Wé's performances on *The Voice* were released on CD and digital download. Wé has also hit the top of the iTunes charts a number of times.

Now, she says, "My life is beautifully hectic." Following her appearance on season 11 of *The Voice*, Wé continues to balance school, vocal training, and professional singing **gigs** all around the nation. She sang the national anthem at the 2017 G'Day USA Awards Show in Hollywood, California, as well as before a New York Knicks game at Madison Square Garden. Later in 2017, she dropped her first single, "Wishes," an original composition that she first preformed on *The Voice*. Wé plans to drop her first Extended Player, or EP, in the summer of 2017.

DID YOU KNOW?

"The Star-Spangled Banner" was written in 1814 by Francis Scott Key and officially became the U.S.'s national anthem in 1931.

Clive Davis

Record producer Clive Davis was born in 1932. For a while, he worked for a law firm that did some work with Columbia Records. He found out that he was more interested in music than law. He took a job with Columbia Records and eventually became president of the company in 1967. He is now the chief creative officer for Sony Music.

Sometimes called "The Man with the Golden Ear," Davis has signed some of the biggest acts in the music business over his long career. He has helped many famous performing artists achieve their goals by mentoring them and shaping their image and sound.

We has continued to focus on her craft as an artist and building her audience.

Being True to Wé

Wé continues to be involved with Harlem School of the Arts. She performs at benefits for the school that helped launch her career. She also recently received the Harlem Stage 2017 Emerging Artist Award. Harlem Stage is a performing arts center that celebrates diversity and the cultural traditions of Harlem. It's no surprise that she received this award. Through her music and her diligence, Wé continues to make her own path through the music industry, honoring herself and Harlem, and offering her gift to the world.

"Success is when you enter this world and make a beautifully large impact, and leave a legacy behind," Wé says. "That doesn't necessarily mean that you have to be a president, a CEO, or a superstar. That means that wherever your world is, [. . .] you should leave an impact there and help change a life at a time even if it's only one. I'm a strong believer in [. . .] manifest[ing] your own dreams. As humans, we are beautiful and powerful people. We have the power to do anything and the talent to create everything. I guess I'm saying, why waste it?"

Make It! HAPPEN!

Record a Demo

To introduce yourself to record labels, you will need to record a "demo." A demo is a rough recording of one to three of your best songs. There are two different ways to record music. One way is track-by-track. This is when each instrument and vocal is recorded separately and then mixed together on music software until all of the levels are at the correct volume. The other way is to do a live recording, where the vocals and the music are recorded at the same time. These days, with a computer and the right software, recording a professional quality demo is not very expensive.

What you will need:

- A computer with a sound card
- At least one microphone
- Headphones
- Music recording software

Record a demo with a friend. How did it turn out? Was it a successful collaboration? How can you improve for your next demo?

Career Spotlights

Wé has been working hard and loving music since she was very young. These are some of the key moments in her career so far.

Amateur Night

In 2015, Wé took the stage at Amateur Night at the Apollo Theater. She crushed it, taking first place twice and placing second overall. She was just 16 years old.

Merit Scholarship

In 2015, Wé received the Clive Davis Future Music Moguls Merit Scholarship, beating out 700 other applicants. She got the chance to see how hit records are made at the Clive Davis Institute of Recorded Music.

The Voice

In 2016, after auditioning in Philadelphia, Pennsylvania, Wé made the cut and became one of the 12 contestants on season 11 of *The Voice*. She went on to become a finalist, getting millions of views on NBC and YouTube.

First Single

Wé's first single, an original song, "Wishes," was released on December 12, 2016. That single performance on *The Voice* has gotten more than 500,000 views on YouTube.

Harlem Stage 2017 Emerging Artist Award

Wé received this award from the respected performing arts center that honors diversity.

Defining Moments

Wé starts singing and acting at the age of four, channeling her energy into the productive development of her skills.

2003

Wé sings at a talent show with her big sister, Jasmine. She is only in third grade. The girls practice a lot and perform "No One" by Alicia Keys.

2007

Wé is bullied in junior high school. For three years, she has no friends.

2009

2012

Wé joins the after-school program at Harlem School of the Arts. There, she practices her singing, makes new friends, and gains many new opportunities to perform at some of New York's most famous concert halls.

2016

Wé is a finalist on *The Voice*, making it into the Top Four and finishing in third place.

2017

Wé receives the key to Paterson, New Jersey, from Mayor Jose Torres.

Depth of Knowledge

1 Wé's father, Mac, has been instrumental to her success. Using the events detailed in the book, answer the following questions: *How did he first inspire her? What milestones has he helped her achieve? How is he currently helping her career?*

2 Bullying is mentioned multiple times throughout the text. Despite the harm it caused Wé as a young adult, how has it seemed to help her achieve success? Use specific examples from the text to support your answer.

3 Wé continues to be challenged by bullying in the music industry, through criticism of her sound and appearance. What skills has she developed that will help her succeed in the face of adversity?

4 What does it take to become a successful performing artist? Talent, skill, hard work, or the right connections? Make a claim and then write an argument to support it, using evidence from this book and other sources.

5 Wé's coach on *The Voice* was Alicia Keys. Conduct a research project to answer the following questions: *When did she get involved in the arts? How did she become famous? What is she doing now to influence society?* Formulate three additional questions about Keys and write an essay answering them.

Record a Talent Show

Collaborate with a group of at least six people to create and record your own talent show like *The Voice*. The work you have done for "Make It Happen!" activity in this book will be helpful.

MATERIALS NEEDED

- Paper and pencils
- Video recording equipment: a video camera, a computer, or a cell phone

STEPS TO TAKE

1   First, plan your talent show. Will it focus on singing, dancing, or other talents? How will contestants be judged? Give all group members a chance to communicate their ideas for the show.

2   Using your group members, fill the roles of contestants, judges, host, and camera operators. Each person's interests and skills should be reflected in their chosen role. Contestants can use the songs they performed for the Chapter 5 "Make It Happen!" feature.

3   Hold a rehearsal. The host should work on their lines, and the contestants should practice their talents.

4   You are ready to film! While the camera operator records, have the host introduce your show. Contestants can perform and judges should provide a critique with positive and constructive criticism.

5   Once you are finished, talk about your roles on the show. What skills enabled you to handle your responsibilities? Review the careers you researched for "Make It Happen!" activity on page 15. Would any group members want to pursue a career in the music industry?

Glossary

amateur *(noun)* a person who does something for pleasure and not as a job (pg. 20)

audition *(noun)* a short performance to show someone's talents (pg. 33)

collaboration *(noun)* to work with another person or group in order to achieve a goal (pg. 6)

communication *(noun)* the act or process of using words, sounds, signs, or behaviors to express or exchange information or to express your ideas, thoughts, feelings, etc., to someone else (pg. 41)

exclude *(verb)* to prevent someone from doing something or being a part of a group (pg. 25)

flexibility *(noun)* willing to change or to try different things (pg. 28)

funk *(noun)* a type of popular music that has a strong beat and combines traditional forms of African American music (such as blues, gospel, or soul) (pg. 13)

gig *(noun)* a job for a musician or actor (pg. 45)

imply *(verb)* to suggest something without saying or showing it plainly (pg. 30)

initiative *(noun)* the determination to learn new things and improve skill levels on your own; the ability to get things done (pg. 6)

jazz *(noun)* a type of American music with lively rhythms and melodies that are often made up by musicians as they play (pg. 9)

mentor *(noun)* someone who teaches or gives help and advice to a less experienced and often younger person (pg. 35)

musical theater *(noun)* a type of play in which singing and dancing play an important part (pg. 17)

orphan *(noun)* a child whose parents are dead (pg. 20)

problem-solving *(noun)* the process or act of finding a solution to a problem (pg. 41)

production *(noun)* a show (such as a play or movie) that is presented to the public (pg. 20)

scholarship *(noun)* an amount of money that is given by a school, an organization, etc., to a student to help pay for the student's education (pg. 41)

self-confidence *(noun)* a feeling of trust in one's abilities, qualities, and judgment (pg. 20)

soul *(noun)* music that combines R&B (rhythm and blues) and gospel music (pg. 11)

syncopated *(adjective)* having a rhythm that stresses the weak beats instead of the strong beats (pg. 30)

tradition *(noun)* a way of thinking, behaving, or doing something that has been used by the people in a particular group, family, society, etc., for a long time (pg. 20)

vocalist *(noun)* a singer (pg. 33)

Read More

Anniss, Matt. *Create Your Own Music.* North Mankato, Minn.: Heinemann-Raintree, 2017.

Becker, Chris. *Freedom of Expression: Interviews with Women in Jazz.* Houston, Tex.: Beckeresque Press, 2015.

Boone, Mary. *Behind-the-Scenes Music Careers.* North Mankato, Minn.: Capstone Press, 2017.

Hill, Z. *B.* Performing Arts. Art Today! Broomall, Pa.: Mason Crest, 2015.

James, Sara. *Writing: Stories, Poetry, Song & Rap.* Art Today! Broomall, Pa.: Mason Crest, 2015.

Pinkney, Andrea Davis. *Rhythm Ride: A Road Trip through the Motown Sound.* New York: Roaring Brook Press, 2015.

Internet Links

www.nbc.com/the-voice

www.rollingstone.com/music/features/amateur-night-at-the-apollo-behind-the-boos-of-americas-toughest-crowd-20150311

www.teenvogue.com/story/we-mcdonald-the-voice-interview

www.encyclopedia.com/people/literature-and-arts/music-popular-and-jazz-biographies/alicia-keys

https://www.youtube.com/watch?v=oSTw1Eji7B8

https://www.youtube.com/watch?v=qlLv5o5Q8Bk

Bibliography

Khoo, Isabelle. "18 Celebrities Share Painful Memories Of Being Bullied In School." *The Huffington Post.* The Huffington Post, 02 Oct. 2015. Web. 19 June 2017.

Rahman, Jayed. "Paterson honors 'Voice' finalist Wé McDonald with citations from mayor, council." *Paterson Times.* N.p., 22 Dec. 2016. Web. 19 June 2017.

Ritz, David. "Soul music." *Encyclopædia Britannica.* Encyclopædia Britannica, Inc., n.d. Web. 19 June 2017.

Weingarten, Christopher R. "Amateur Night at the Apollo: Behind the Boos." *Rolling Stone.* Rolling Stone, 11 Mar. 2015. Web. 19 June 2017.

Wiest, Brianna. "'The Voice' Singer Wé McDonald on Alicia Keys and Her Music Idols." *Teen Vogue.* TeenVogue.com, 25 May 2017. Web. 19 June 2017.

Wills, Cheryl. "Meet 'The Voice' Contestant Wé McDonald." *Essence.com.* Essence. com, 25 Oct. 2016. Web. 06 July 2017.

"Wé McDonald talks about performing and songs her father used to play in the house." *YouTube.* YouTube, 13 Oct. 2016. Web. 06 July 2017.

"Wé McDonald's dad on preparing for 'The Voice' finale." *North Jersey.* N.p., n.d. Web. 06 July 2017.

Index